ff
p
poco a poco cresc.
ossia
poco rit. a tempo
f
poco a poco cresc.
cresc.
f
poco a poco dim.
poco a poco cresc.
f
ff

Some time ago in another country, there lived a king who had eight fiddlers, a wise cat named Joachim, so many accountants they couldn't be counted—and hardly any money.

The palace roof was full of holes; jewels kept dropping off the King's crown, and he could never afford to make fires in his sixty-six fireplaces. But none of this seemed to matter.

Joachim was a fine fiddler himself, being distantly related to that famous fiddle-playing cat who made the cow jump over the moon. Sometimes he played the ninth violin in the King's little orchestra.

"A king with fiddlers is worth more than money in the bank," was a saying in that country, where the people loved beautiful music and happy sayings.

When his little orchestra played, the King opened his palace to all

his subjects who came to listen, to sing, and to dance.

Someone always brought wood for the fire. When a jewel fell out of the King's crown everybody got down on hands and knees and searched for it. When the rain leaked through the palace roof people simply opened their umbrellas and went on listening to the music.

Well, everyone that is, except the King's accountants. They were too busy counting the holes in the roof, the jewels tumbling from the King's crown, and the cold fireplaces. But mostly they counted the King's money and each time they counted, there was less of it. The only thing the accountants weren't good at counting was themselves.

Oh, many, many times the accountants tried to count themselves. One said, ''We must begin by counting each other's pencils.'' Another said, ''No, no, I say we must start by counting all the adding machines. . . .''

Still another suggested that they count each other's rulers and divide by the number of erasers. Finally, the King decided that he would count the accountants himself.

The great counting took place in the Royal Ballroom. The King and Joachim took their places on the dais and the King's eight fiddlers played military marches while the accountants filed into the Ballroom. It was a very noisy business. There was the ringing of the adding machines, the click of the abaci, the scratch of pencils, and the King's little string orchestra could barely be heard.

The King's counting, however, went no better. Although he was careful to write down all his subtotals, and he always remembered to carry his tens, he came up with a different answer each time he counted his accountants. First there were fifty-nine, then there were seventy-two and then there were ninety-eight.

And all the time icy rainwater leaked through a hole in the palace roof and trickled down the King's neck.

"Why can't I count my accountants?" he wailed.

"Because, Sire," Joachim whispered in the royal ear, "each time you count them there are more of them."

The King was bewildered and cold. He gave a shiver because the Royal Ballroom was without a fire. ''Why do I have so many accountants?''

Joachim smoothed his whiskers. ''To help you keep track of your money.''

''But I have hardly any money.''

''I don't understand why it should be so, Sire,'' Joachim replied, ''but the less money you have, the more accountants you seem to need to tell you how to save what little money you have.''

At the mention of saving money the Chief Accountant stepped forward with a low bow and gave the King an extremely clever smile. ''Answer me one question, Sire. What are your musicians doing at the moment?''

The King looked over at his little band of fiddlers. ''Why, they're playing their violins, of course.''

"Exactly!" said the Chief Accountant. "That's the
trouble with fiddlers. Even when they're working,
they're really only playing. If you want to save money, fire
them and you will have enough to mend your roof, repair
your crown, and make fires in all sixty-six fireplaces."

The King was deeply shocked. Dismiss his fiddlers?
All kings have fiddlers. Why, Louis the Fourteenth of
France had twenty-four. And even Old King Cole, who
never had much money, kept three. . . . But the King was
cold and wet, and a damp king is easily tempted. ''I shall
have to consult my cat,'' he said.

Joachim looked up at the King with his brilliant green
eyes and recited a saying very popular among his
countrymen:
''*Better a cold fireplace than a king without fiddlers.*''

''I'm tired of sayings,'' said the King grumpily,
''and I'm tired of leaks in the roof and cold fireplaces,
and the more I think about it, the more sense the Chief
Accountant makes and—oh, drat!''—he exclaimed
as a large ruby dropped from his crown and rolled
under the throne.

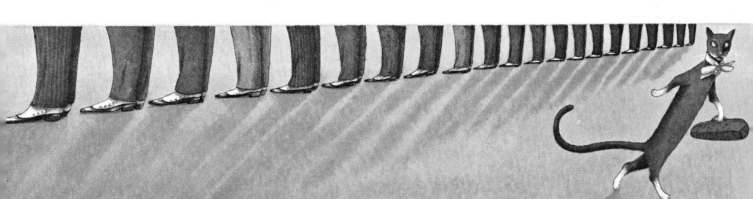

That was the last straw.

Down on his hands and knees, scrabbling under his throne for the jewel, the King gave the order:

''Dismiss the fiddlers!''

And all the accountants cheered and waved their worksheets.

No one noticed Joachim, who slipped from the dais like a swift, sleek shadow and disappeared.

At first it really did seem that all the Chief Accountant had promised was coming true. With the money he saved the King had his roof fixed, paid for the wood for fires in all sixty-six fireplaces, re-set the gleaming jewels in his crown, and felt very pleased with himself indeed.

Of Joachim there was no sign. The King searched
for him in all his favorite places: in the Royal Linen
Cupboard, on the orchard wall, and on his favorite
branch of the pomegranate tree. But Joachim had
vanished without a trace.

Gradually things began to change in the kingdom. Because
there was no music, the people became depressed and
began to argue over everything.

They even began to make up sad sayings like:
"A palace without music is like a hive without honey."

And nobody came to visit the King anymore, even though the accountants said he could invite the people to listen to them work. All the palace servants developed bad tempers, and when the King tried to hum a little tune to cheer himself up, it was almost drowned out by the sound of footmen quarreling in the corridors, royal pages fighting in their bedrooms, and soldiers grumbling on the battlements. It was about this time that the King made up a saying of his own:

"*Better a damp monarch than an empty court.*"

And all who heard it thoroughly agreed.

One evening the King went to bed early with a terrible headache. He couldn't sleep so he tried counting sheep, but the sheep turned into accountants.

It was well past midnight before the King finally fell asleep and in the very early hours of the morning he was woken up by the sound of someone playing the violin very beautifully. Putting on his gown and slippers and taking a candle, the King padded through the silent corridors to the Royal Ballroom. There on the dais was Joachim with his fiddle beneath his chin.

"Your Majesty, I have roamed the world, deep in thought, and I have found the answer to your problems!" And to celebrate he played a little jig while the King danced around the ballroom.

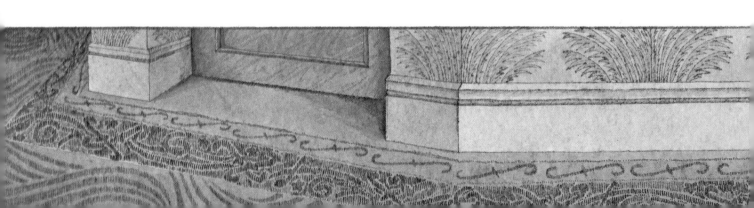

"If you wish to give music back to your people—"

"Yes!" said the King loudly.

"—if you wish to have singing and dancing in your palace again—"

"Yes!" said the King, even more loudly.

"—then, Sire," said Joachim, "you must learn to make music yourself."

"But I can't play anything," wailed the King.

"Oh, but you will, and I, Joachim, will teach you. As for your accountants, you must pass a law that from now on all Royal Accountants must also play a musical instrument."

Joachim patted the King on the knee. "Do not worry, Sire, leave everything to me."

The very next day Joachim began to teach the King how to play the violin.

"A good fiddler must learn special exercises," said Joachim, "every part of his body must work in perfect coordination: the head and the heart, the neck and the knees, the feet and the fingers . . . all must work happily together."

"Together?" said the King who was still doubtful. "Yes, *together*," replied Joachim, "to get the music out."

Joachim's special exercises for learning the violin began.

First there were Windmills, which helped the King to relax. Then came the Balloon, which required the King to inhale as much air as possible. Next came some headstands, to loosen the muscles of the neck. Many more exercises followed with odd names like Putting Up the Violin and the Golf Swing. . . .

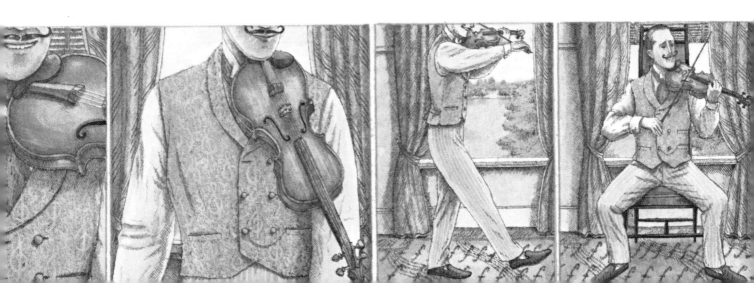

At first the King made many mistakes.
He dropped his violin under his chin so that it looked like he was growing a beard. He gripped his bow fiercely in what Joachim called the Frozen Spider and the sounds he made were so awful that people passing the palace thought they heard something like silk tearing, and cats fighting, and babies crying all at once.

The accountants were horrified by the King's new law. "I prefer addition," said one. "Subtraction," said the next. "Long division," said another.

It was only when Joachim explained to them that counting time played a very important role in music that they agreed to try. And then they did very well; the only trouble was that they preferred counting aloud and when a group of accountants begins counting aloud it can be difficult to hear the music. Some of them enjoyed the counting so much that they forgot to play at all.

But the King grew better and better. Eventually, the great day came when Joachim pronounced him good enough to be heard in public. "I have brought music back to you," Joachim told him, "now you must give the music back to your people."

The King went on the road with Joachim as his
manager. Slowly the country began to sing and dance
again. What began as a one-man band soon grew.
When the butcher's boy asked if he could take lessons, the
King had a duo; and when the milkman expressed an
interest they formed a trio; and when the Chief of Soldiers
asked if he could play too, the King had a quartet.

And all the poor fiddlers the King had fired came back too.
And so they went, the King and his strolling musicians,
playing in towns and villages, in hospitals, churches,
factories, and farmyards under Joachim's flashing baton,
until there wasn't a soul left in all the kingdom who
hadn't heard or seen the King, the cat, and the fiddle.

Meanwhile, back in the palace, fingers that had never tapped anything other than an adding machine became acquainted with the piano, the clarinet, the cello, the trumpet, and the drums. Before long the palace had its own Royal Philharmonic Orchestra composed entirely of accountants. Perhaps most surprising of all, the Chief Accountant himself, after years of fiddling with figures, proved rather good at fiddling with the fiddle. So good in fact that eventually he was second only to the King himself.

And so once again, just as it had been in the old days, the King's palace was alive with music, singing, and dancing. The people packed into the Royal Ballroom for the grand concerts with Joachim upon the rostrum and the King leading the violins. The audience would look up to where the Chief Accountant sat beside the King and they would recite a saying often heard since Joachim brought music back to the country:

"Happy is the kingdom where the accountant plays second fiddle

to the King."

Ten Little Exercises
for Kings, Accountants, and Other Young Violinists.

1. WINDMILLS

a. Arms and legs are stretched
   and pointed away from each other.

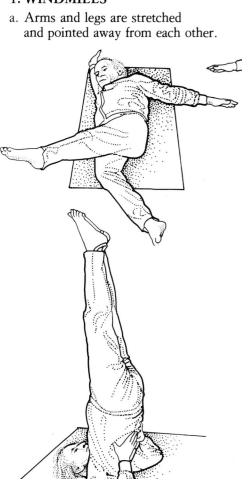

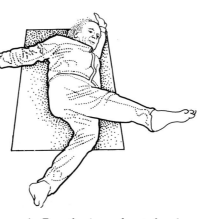

b. Breathe in and out deeply
   while rolling rhythmically
   from side to side.

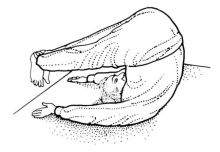

2. THE PLOUGH

A good way of loosening
up before practising.

3. THE SHOULDER STAND

Far easier than the head stand.

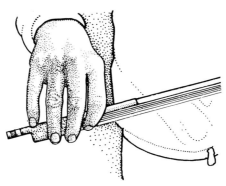

4. TAKING UP THE BOW

a. Take up the bow as gently
   as you would a little bird.

   See how lightly the little
   finger rests.

b. The correct position
   of the thumb.

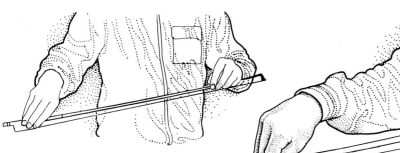

5. PUSH-PULL

a. Taking the bow in the correct
   hold gently push it through
   the fingers of the left hand.

b. The shape of the hand at
   the start of the push.

c. At the end of the pull.

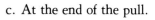

6. SHOOTING THE BOW

a. Fiddle is tucked into neck and rests along the arm.

b. As the bow begins to move, the left hand steadies the fiddle.

c. Bow goes shooting off the strings and keeps on going as far as possible.

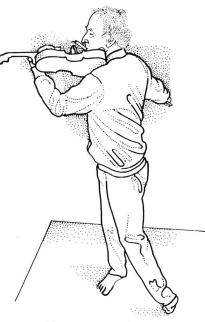

7. THE GOLF SWING

a. Put up the bow.

b. Swing your body to the right, as far as you can.

c. Turn on your feet like a golfer. Do the same to the left.

8. VIBRATIONS

a. Stretch your fingers as far as you can towards the bridge.

b. Move up the neck of the violin lightly pressing one, two, or more fingers on the string.

c. Feel the vibrations flowing through you.

~Allegro~

violon

J.H. Fiocco

Arrangée par
Arthur Bent & Norman O'?